POEMS about the SEASIDE

WAYLAND
www.waylandbooks.co.uk

First published in Great Britain in 2015 by Wayland

Editor: Victoria Brooker
Designer: Lisa Peacock

ISBN: 978 0 7502 9175 0
Library eBook ISBN: 978 0 7502 9176 7

10 9 8 7 6 5 4 3 2 1

Wayland, an imprint of Hachette Children's Group
Part of Hodder & Stoughton
Carmelite House
50 Victoria Embankment
London EC4Y 0DZ

An Hachette UK Company
www.hachette.co.uk
www.hachettechildrens.co.uk

Printed and bound in China

Acknowledgements:
The Compiler and Publisher would like to thank the authors for allowing their poems to appear in
this anthology. Poems © the authors. While every attempt has been made to gain permissions and
provide an up-to-date biography, in some cases this has not been possible and we apologise for
any omissions. Should there be any inadvertent omission, please apply to the Publisher for rectification.

All websites were valid at the time of going to press. However, it is possible that some addresses may have changed or
closed down since publication. While the Publisher and Compiler regret any inconvenience this may cause the readers,
no responsiblity for any such changes can be accepted by either the Compiler or the Publisher.

FSC
www.fsc.org

MIX
Paper from
responsible sources
FSC® C104740

Contents

Are We Nearly There Yet? *by Brian Moses*............................4

Beach Counting *by Tony Mitton*................................6

I Do Like to be Beside the Seaside *by John A. Glover-Kind*... 8

The Seagull's Song *by June Crebbin*............................9

Seagulls With Everything *by Brian Moses*........................10

Seaside Sounds *by John Foster*.................................12

A Single Wave *by Ian Souter*..................................14

The 7th Wave *by Jan Dean*.....................................15

There's An Ocean in this Seashell *by Graham Denton*.........16

Shells *by Debra Bertulis*.......................................17

Skimming Stones on the Sea *by Jane Clarke*....................18

Treasure Chest Mystery *by Kate Williams*...............19

Playtime Pirate (Action Rhyme) *by Tony Mitton*......20

Letters in Bottles *by Clare Bevan*......................... ..22

The Bucket *by James Carter*.................................24

Rock Pool *by Matt Goodfellow*...........................26

The Friendly Octopus *by Mike Jubb*.......................27

Crab *by Irene Assiba D'Almeida*.........................28

Man on the Beach *by Joshua Seigal*................29

Further information.................30

Index of first lines..................31

Are We Nearly There Yet?

When we went to the seaside this year
my little sister just wouldn't be quiet.

Again and again
she kept on asking,
"Are we nearly there yet?"

We drove to the end of our street
and my sister said,
"Are we nearly there yet?"

We left the town behind
and again she said,
"Are we nearly there yet?"

We stopped for a train to go by
and my sister called,
"Are we nearly there yet?"

We sped along the motorway
and my sister said,
"Are we nearly there yet?"

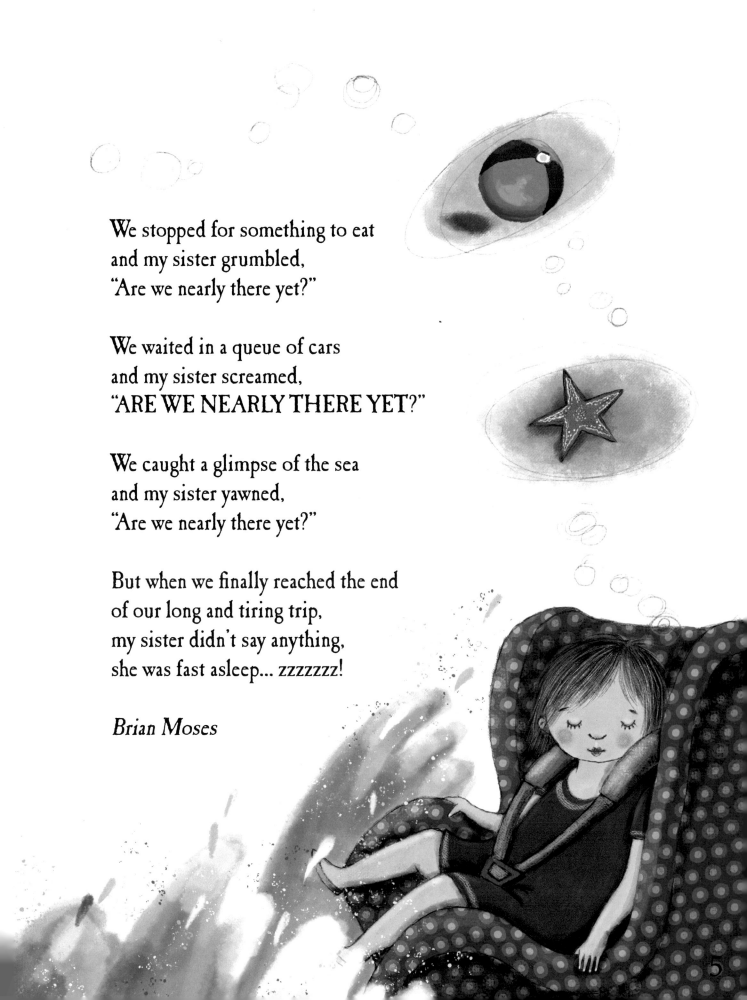

We stopped for something to eat
and my sister grumbled,
"Are we nearly there yet?"

We waited in a queue of cars
and my sister screamed,
"ARE WE NEARLY THERE YET?"

We caught a glimpse of the sea
and my sister yawned,
"Are we nearly there yet?"

But when we finally reached the end
of our long and tiring trip,
my sister didn't say anything,
she was fast asleep... zzzzzzz!

Brian Moses

Beach Counting

One for the sun that shone in the sky.

Two for the ships that sailed on by.

Three for the castles I built on the sand.

Four for the seashells I held in my hand.

Five for the points on the starfish I saw.

Six for the crabs that scuttled ashore.

Seven for the waves that I managed to beat.

Eight for the pebbles I perched on my feet.

Nine for the boats that bobbed on the sea.

Ten for my toes that were wiggling free.

Tony Mitton

I Do Like to be Beside the Seaside

Oh! I do like to be beside the seaside
I do like to be beside the sea
I do like to stroll upon the Prom, Prom, Prom,
Where the brass bands play
Tiddely om pom pom!
So just let me be beside the seaside
I'll be beside myself with glee
And there's lots of girls beside,
I should like to be beside,
Beside the seaside!
Beside the sea!

John A. Glover-Kind

The Seagull's Song

Oh! I do like to be beside the seaside
I do like to be beside the sea,
I do like to soar above a seaside town,
See the boats in the harbour bobbing up and down.

Oh! I do like to be beside the seaside
There is nowhere that I would rather be,
I can perch on sailing ships,
Grab a meal of fish and chips,
Beside the seaside, beside the sea.

June Crebbin

Seagulls With Everything

You get seagulls with everything
at St Ives...

Seagulls with walking sticks,
seagulls with glasses,
seagulls with lipstick
and ones with moustaches.

Seagulls with hats
to cover bald heads,
seagulls with duvets
still lying in bed.

Seagulls with tickets
to travel on trains,
seagulls with telescopes
high up on cranes.

Seagulls with lollies
and ice cream cones,
seagulls with diaries
and mobile phones.

Seagulls in shades
strumming guitars,
seagulls with girlfriends
driving fast cars.

Seagulls with dreams
to fly from St Ives
and be big movie stars
for the rest of their lives.

Brian Moses

11

Seaside Sounds

Listen can you hear
    The whisper of the waves brushing the shore
The slip-slop of the flip-flops on the sand
    The fluttering of the flag flapping in the breeze
The splish-splosh of water slopping from a child's bucket
    The raucous squawks of the marauding seagulls
The cries and gasps of bathers as the cold water swirls around them
    The screams and howls as they splash each other
The warning shout of a mother.
    The sobbing of the child who has dropped her ice-cream.
Grandad's snore as he sleeps in his deckchair.

John Foster

A Single Wave

A single wave
knows just how to behave!

A swish,
a swash
and a swoosh of a leap
then a graceful, white curtsey
performed gently at your feet.

Yes a single wave
knows just how to behave!

Ian Souter

The 7th Wave

first wave   slops slow
hop-step   come-go

second wave pushes
shoves and rushes

wave number three
picks on me

wave four
is all roar

wave five is a breaker
a crashing breath-taker

wave six rises high
is a green and salty sky

the seventh wave's a slammer
a roller-rock-rammer
a beach-bashing
shell-smashing
monster-sized
hammer

Jan Dean

There's An Ocean In This Seashell

There's an ocean in this seashell
That I'm holding to my ear.
As I listen very closely
It's an ocean I can hear.
It is swishing, it is swashing,
It is sloshing all about.
It is splashing, it is thrashing,
It is dashing in and out.

There's an ocean in this seashell,
But wherever can it be?
When I look inside this seashell
There is nothing there to see.
Yet I know it was an ocean
For I heard its mighty roar,
As I listened to this seashell
That I found upon the shore.

Graham Denton

Shells

White ones
Pink ones
Rough and smooth and shiny ones,
Big ones,
Small ones
Long and thin and tiny ones
Dust off the sand!
Wash them in the sea!
A bucket full of memories
Coming home with me.

Debra Bertulis

Skimming Stones on the Sea

When the sea shimmers still and grey
It's a perfect skim stone day.

Choose a stone that's flat and thin,
Frisbee it and watch it skim.

Skip

skip

skip.

Skip,

skip,

skip,

PLOP!

Count the ripples of each hop.

It's a perfect skim stone day
when the sea shimmers still and grey.

Jane Clarke

18

Treasure Chest Mystery

What could be in the treasure chest,
forgotten at the bottom of the sea?

A diamond ring?
A fine silk scarf?
A bottle of rum to make the sailors laugh?
A silver sword?
A golden crown?
A crumpled map, all soggy and brown?

A beautiful bracelet, blue as the sky?
An old peg-leg?
A patch for an eye?

A wishing-well of wonders
there could be,
forgotten at the bottom of the sea!

Kate Williams

Playtime Pirate (Action Rhyme)

This is my treasure map.   (make map with 2 hands)
This is my boat.   (draw boat around body)
These are the waves   (make wave motions with hands on both sides)
where I rock and float.

There is the island   (point to island in distance)
I'm headed for.
This is the way   (mime wading through shallows)
that I wade ashore.

This is the spot.   (draw X in front of self, pointing to ground)
This is my spade.   (grip mimed spade)
This is the deep,   (dig with mimed spade)
dark hole I made.

This is the box   (lift mimed box from hole)
that I dug from the ground.
And these are the golden   (fling coins into the air with glee)
coins I found.

Tony Mitton

Letters in Bottles

I'm stranded on an island.
There's no one else. Just me.
But PLEASE don't send a
rescue ship –
I'm as happy as can be.

In the Under-Sea Museum
(Below the deepest wave)
You'll find a THOUSAND bottles
In a sleepy, creepy cave.
And EACH ONE holds a letter
That was written long ago –
What happened to the writers?
I'm afraid we'll never know ...

Across the seas
This note has come.
I'm safe. I'm well.
Please tell my Mum.

Dear Reader,
In your salty hand
You hold a map —
It shows a land
Where TREASURE lies
Beneath the sand.
The X will show you
Where to look. Good luck!
Good digging!
From: C. Hook.

I'm tired. I'm bored.
I'm on a boat,
And all we do
ALL DAY is float.
So here's a note
From me to you.
(The date is 1892.)

You've found my letter!
Write back soon —
This morning, or
This afternoon.
I'll wait. I'll watch
The stormy seas.
I'm VERY lonely.
Write back! Please!

Clare Bevan

23

The Bucket

Do you remember
that afternoon, dashing
across the sand? Bucket
in hand, net in the other,
then hovering over
every pool? And once
we'd done, hurrying back,
bucket now full, everyone
trying to catch a glimpse
of three green crabs,
two little fish,
and all of those
fidgety shrimps?

Then finally strolling
back to sea, wading out,
T-shirts wet, tipping
them into the waves?
How could we
ever forget?

James Carter

25

Rock Pool

Barnacle's on bass guitar,
hermit-crab on drums,
starfish does the singing
and a shrimp guitarist strums.

The hardest rockin' group around,
come catch us, playing live —
but get your ticket quick because
we tour on every tide!

Matt Goodfellow

26

The Friendly Octopus

Eight arms for me, eight arms for me,
I'm a friendly octopus, under the sea.

I've got

One arm to blow my nose,
One arm to wave with,
One arm to brush my teeth,
One arm to shave with,
One arm to comb my hair,
One arm to shake with,
One arm to blow a kiss,
And one to eat a cake with.

Eight arms for me, eight arms for me,
I'm a friendly octopus, under the sea.

Mike Jubb

27

Crab

Crab with a small brain
      Why do you
Go backward
      To go forward?
Is it my own world
      Is it your own world
Which is upside down?
      Lucky you are not a car
Otherwise
      Oh dear, oh dear
You would have so many accidents!

Irene Assiba D'Almeida

28

Man on the Beach

Where is he going?
Where has he been?
Where does he come from?
What has he seen?
Why is he limping?
Is he in pain?
Why is he walking
alone in the rain?
Does he feel jolly?
Does he feel sad?
Does he have children?
Is he a dad?
Are his hands freezing?
Is his coat warm?
Why is he walking
alone in the storm?

Joshua Seigal

Further information

Once a poem in this book has been read, either individually, in groups, or by the parent or teacher, check with the children that they have understood what the poem is about. Ask them to point out any difficult lines or words and explain these. Ask the children how they feel about the poem. Do they like it? Is there a certain section or line of the poem that they particularly enjoy?

'Are We Nearly There Yet?' by Brian Moses is a poem for performance. Different children can speak the verses while a group of children call out the chorus. It can be spoken in different ways in appropriate places - grumbled, shouted, whispered etc. Further verses could be written by children and added to the poem -

"We were delayed by roadworks
and my sister yelled out,
"Are we nearly there yet?"

Tony Mitton's 'Beach Counting' is a poem for reading aloud. Children can also write their own counting poems in this way. Make a list of lots of other items that can be found on the beach, or at a harbour, or on a pier. Children may enjoy listening to a musical version of 'I do like to be beside the seaside' and again, it would be perfect for performance at an assembly or school music hall. Some could work on the original version and others on the alternative version, 'The Seagull's Song' by June Crebbin.

'Seagulls With Everything' by Brian Moses could act as a model poem for children's own ideas. How about 'Crabs with Everything' or a mix of 'Sea Creatures with Everything'?

John Foster's poem 'Seaside Sounds' would prove particularly useful for children on a school trip to the beach where they could identify the sounds that John heard in his poem. They can then 'collect' their own sounds, smells or sights for poems of their own.

Compare the poems by Ian Souter and Jan Dean. Both are about waves on the seashore and were probably written from first-hand observation. Again, a trip to the beach could get children looking at the waves themselves and thinking of 'movement' words to describe how they behave.

Graham Denton's 'There's an Ocean in This Seashell' poem reminds us about holding a shell to the ear and hearing the sound of the ocean. What else might children hear in their shells? In 'Shells' by Debra Bertulis, Debra writes about shells collected from the beach. She describes them as a 'bucket full of memories'. Children could find their own shells or work with a collection in the classroom and imagine where each one was found.

Jane Clarke's poem 'Skimming Stones on the Sea' is an example of a poem where the words form a picture. Show children other examples of shape poems like this and talk about which ones work the best. Children can add to the contents of Kate Williams' treasure chest. Maybe they could make a model chest to use in a performance of Tony Mitton's action rhyme 'Playtime Pirate.'

'Letters in Bottles' by Clare Bevan will inspire children to imagine that they too are stranded on an island. What would they say in a letter to go in a bottle? 'The Bucket' by James Carter will encourage the sharing of children's own memories of trips to the seaside. They could write them in a similar way beginning, as James does, with 'Do you remember?'

Matt Goodfellow's 'Rock Pool' is a fun poem to learn. It could also be extended with other creatures playing different instruments. 'The Friendly Octopus' by Mike Jubb is another action rhyme that children will enjoy learning and performing.

Irene Assiba D'Almeida asks a question of her 'Crab'. This is a good way of beginning a poem about a seashore creature.

Are there stars in your eyes
starfish,
when you look to the sky
at night?

'Man on the Beach' by Joshua Seigal is a poem composed entirely of questions. Again an effective model poem when writing about creatures or people.

Encourage children to look for further examples of poems about the seaside. These can be copied out and then illustrated. Build up a collection of poems and let children talk about their favourites. Let them practise reading and performing the poems adding actions and percussion accompaniment if appropriate.

About the Poets:

Clare Bevan used to be a teacher until she decided to become a writer instead. So far, she has written stories, plays, song lyrics, picture books and a huge heap of poetry. Her poems have appeared in over one hundred anthologies, and she loves performing them in schools. Her hobbies are reading and acting, and she once dressed up as a farmyard chicken.

Debra Bertulis' life-long passion is the written and spoken word, and she is the author of many published poems for children. She is regularly invited into schools where her workshops inspire pupils to compose and perform their own poetry. Debra lives in Herefordshire where she enjoys walking the nearby Welsh hills and seeking out second-hand book shops! www.debrabertulis.com

James Carter is the liveliest children's poet and guitarist in town. He's travelled nearly everywhere from Loch Ness to Southern Spain with his guitar, Keith, to give performances and workshops in schools and libraries and also festivals. An award-winning poet, his titles are published by Frances Lincoln, Macmillan and Bloomsbury. Find him, read him, hear him at: www.jamescarterpoet.co.uk

Jane Clarke is the author of over 80 children's books including the award-winning picture books *Stuck in the Mud*, illustrated by Gary Parsons, and *Gilbert the Great*, illustrated by Charles Fuge. She's delighted to have a poem in this anthology. www.jane-clarke.co.uk

Jan Dean likes ice cream and earrings. Her penguin earrings are special favourites. (Also the giraffes.) She likes singing, drawing and making bread. She visits schools to perform her poems and write new poems with classes. She likes it best when the poems explode all over the whiteboards and dribble down the walls... www.jandean.co.uk

Graham Denton is a writer and anthologist of poetry for children, whose poems feature in numerous publications both in the UK and abroad. As an anthologist, his compilations include *Orange Silver Sausage: A Collection of Poems Without Rhymes* (Walker Books), *My Cat is in Love with The Goldfish* (A & C Black) and *When Granny Won Olympic Gold* (A&C Black). Most recently, Graham celebrated the release of the first full collection of his own funny verses, *My Rhino Plays The Xylophone*, published by A&C Black. He has also twice been short listed for the UK's CLPE Poetry Award.

John Foster is a children's poet, anthologist and poetry performer, well-known for his performance as a dancing dinosaur. He has written over 1,500 poems and *The Poetry Chest* containing over 250 of his own poems is published by Oxford University Press. He is a former teacher and the author of many books for classroom use. www.johnfosterchildrenspoet.co.uk

Matt Goodfellow is a poet and primary school teacher from Manchester. His poems have been published in magazines and anthologies worldwide. Matt's high-energy performances and workshops have delighted, excited and enthused thousands of children in schools, libraries and bookshops across the UK. www.mattgoodfellow.yolasite.com

Mike Jubb's poems are widely anthologised and he has a picture book, *Splosh,* published by Scholastic.

Tony Mitton has been published as a poet for children since the early '90s. He has also written many successful verse picture books and works blending poetry with narrative. He has won several awards. He lives in Cambridge where he continues to read and write. www.tonymitton.co.uk

Brian Moses lives in Burwash in Sussex where the famous writer Rudyard Kipling once lived. He travels the country performing his poetry and percussion show in schools, libraries and theatres. He has published more than 200 books including the series of picture books *Dinosaurs Have Feelings Too* (Wayland). His favourite animal is his fox red labrador, Honey. www.brianmoses.co.uk

Joshua Seigal is a poet, performer and educator who works with children of all ages and abilities. He has performed his poems at schools, libraries and festivals around the country, as well as leading workshops designed to inspire confidence and creativity. He has been described by teachers as 'inspirational' and 'a positive male role model'. www.joshuaseigal.co.uk

Ian Souter is retired from teaching and loves to exercise, play music and travel. He lives in the wilds of Surrey but also loves to visit, in particular, France and Australia. On his travels he also keeps an eye (and an ear) open for words and ideas. Sometimes he finds them hanging from trees or people's mouths or even sparkling in the sunshine.

Kate Williams When Kate's children were young, she made up poems to read them at bedtime. It was their clever idea that she send them off to a publisher, and she's been contributing to children's anthologies ever since! Kate finds writing a poem is like making a collage, but less sticky – except that she's stuck in the craze! She provides workshops for schools, too. www.poemsforfun.wordpress.com

Index of first lines

When we went to the seaside this year........................4

One for the sun that shone in the sky......................... 6

Oh! I do like to be beside the seaside......................... 8

Oh! I do like to be beside the seaside......................... 9

You get seagulls with everything................................ 10

Listen can you hear.. 12

A single wave knows just how to behave.....................14

first wave slops slow..15

There's an ocean in this seashell................................ 16

White ones...17

When the sea shimmers still and grey........................ 18

What could be in the treasure chest........................... 19

This is my treasure map.. 20

I'm stranded on an island.. 22

Do you remember.. 24

Barnacle's on bass guitar... 26

Eight arms for me, eight arms for me......................... 27

Crab with a small brain... 28

Where is he going?.. 29

Titles in the series:

Poems About Festivals:
978 0 7502 9184 2

Let's Celebrate by Sue Hardy-Dawson
The Chinese Dragon by Catherine Benson
Pancake Day by Debra Bertulis
Holi, Festival of Colour by Punitha Perinparaja
Mother's Day by Eric Finney
Children's Day by Penny Kent
Eid-ul-Fitr by Penny Kent
It's Diwali Tonight by John Foster
Harvest Thanks by Jan Dean
A Hallowe'en Pumpkin by Dorothy Aldis
Fireworks by Judith Nicholls
Eight Candles Burning by Celia Warren
Long, Long Ago
Christmas Eve by Brian Moses
Happy New Year by Brenda Williams

Poems About Seasons:
978 0 7502 9181 1

Spring Phoned by Ian Souter
Spring by Clare Bevan
Springtime in Bluebell Wood by Wes Magee
Spring in the City by Brian Moses
What is Summer For? by Kate Williams
Summer Clouds by Penny Kent
Bed in Summer by R.L. Stevenson
Dear Summer by Kenn Nesbitt
The Swallow by Christina Rossetti
Autumn? by Chris White
Autumn Song by John Rice
Autumn Action Rhyme by Tony Mitton
Sounds Like Winter by Chris White
I Hear Thunder
December by Daphne Kitching
Mr Snowman by Debra Bertulis
Snow Joke by Clare Bevan
The Seasons in Me by Jane Clarke
Time by Trevor Harvey

Poems About Animals:
978 0 7502 9178 1

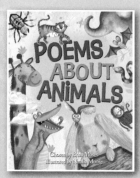

The Terrible Ten by James Carter
On My Way From School by Roger Stevens
Animal Riddles by Marian Swinger
My Dog by Joshua Seigal
Sad Rabbit by Eric Finney
A Bear in his Underwear by Brian Moses
Komodo Dragon by Graham Denton
I'm a Giraffe by Mike Jubb
Hungry Crocodile by Carol Rumble
If You Should Meet a Crocodile
How to Spot a Kangaroo by Robert Scotallero
Caterpillar by Christina Rossetti
Swish Swash by Bill Condon
Tiger by Alison Chisholm
Animal Farewells by Kate Snow

Poems About the Seaside:
978 0 7502 9175 0

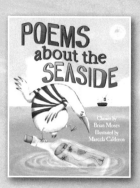

Are We Nearly There Yet? by Brian Moses
Beach Counting by Tony Mitton
I Do Like to be Beside the Seaside by John A. Glover-Kind
The Seagull's Song by June Crebbin
Seagulls With Everything by Brian Moses
Seaside Sounds by John Foster
A Single Wave by Ian Souter
The 7th Wave by Jan Dean
There's an Ocean in This Seashell by Graham Denton
Shells by Debra Bertulis
Skimming Stones on the Sea by Jane Clarke
Treasure Chest Mystery by Kate Williams
Playtime Pirate (Action Rhyme) by Tony Mitton
Letters in Bottles by Clare Bevan
The Bucket by James Carter
Rock Pool by Matt Goodfellow
The Friendly Octopus by Mike Jubb
Crab by Irene Assiba D'Almeida
Man on the Beach by Joshua Seigal